Survivors
White Water Rafting

John Goodwin

Published in association with
The Basic Skills Agency

Hodder Murray
A MEMBER OF THE HODDER HEADLINE GROUP

Orders: please contact Bookpoint Ltd, 130 Milton Park, Abingdon, Oxon OX14 4SB. Telephone: (44) 01235 827720. Fax: (44) 01235 400454. Lines are open 9.00–6.00, Monday to Saturday, with a 24-hour message answering service. Visit our website at www.hoddereducation.co.uk

© John Goodwin 2005
First published in 2005 by
Hodder Murray, a member of the Hodder Headline Group
338 Euston Road
London NW1 3BH

Impression number   10 9 8 7 6 5 4 3 2 1
Year   2010 2009 2008 2007 2006 2005

Cover photo © The Image Bank/Getty Images.
Inside illustrations Gary Andrews.
Typeset by Transet Limited, Coventry, England.
Printed in Great Britain by Athenaeum Press Ltd, Gateshead, Tyne & Wear.

A catalogue record for this title is available from the British Library

ISBN-10: 0 340 90067 9
ISBN-13: 978 0 340 90067 3

Contents

1

Our rubber raft spun round and round.
Then it turned wildly.
The white water all around us hissed in fury.
It roared over rocks
and swirled madly in whirlpools.
It rose in the air in giant sprays.

I gripped my paddle as tight
as I could with both hands.
I tried to see what was
round the next bend in the river.
Could it be an even worse rapid?
A giant waterfall?
Fallen tree trunks?

The river pulled us on.
It was like a wild animal with white fangs.
Sharp rocks for its teeth.
It was a water belly that changed
every time you looked at it.
It had whirlpool eyes
and a roaring voice.
Foaming breath that burned.

Jez was in the raft with me.
My worst nightmare.
And his.

'Oh, no,' said Jez.
'I don't want Fleahead.
Why can't I be with Lucy?
She's my best mate.
I don't mind Tariq or Ben.
But not Fleahead.
No way,' he said.

But Watson our instructor wouldn't listen.
'It's not your choice, Jez.
You'll go with Fleahead and that's it.'

But Watson was wrong.
It wasn't the end of it at all.
Oh no.
Just the beginning.

Jez had to have the best helmet
and the biggest paddle.
He had to choose the smartest raft
and the best life jacket.
And he had to sit in the front of the raft.

Then he ignored me.
It was like I didn't exist.

He waved wildly
at all the others in their rafts.
He shouted and laughed.
He sang all the time.
In fact, he sang so loudly that
even the roar of the water
couldn't drown him out.

His singing really got to me.
Big time.

Why are you such a pain, Jez?
When are you going to grow up?

We rounded the bend in the river.
More rapids ahead.
White water all around us.
I was trapped in with loudmouth.
There was no way out.

I closed my eyes and gripped my paddle.
Somehow we got through all the rapids.
But I never wanted to do it again.
Please.
Never, ever again.

2

'All of you managed the rapids.
You've now done the first part
of the rafting challenge,' said Watson.
'But the next part is going to be harder.
Much harder.'

He led us away from the white water.
We walked to a different part of the river.
We came to two brown muddy pools
with no racing current.

'I thought you said it was going
to be harder,' sneered Jez.
'It is,' said Watson, folding his arms.
'How come?' said Jez.
'Because now you have to build
your own raft,' said Watson.

He then pointed to two piles
of big blue plastic barrels.
Beside them were wooden planks
and bundles of thick rope.
'These are the materials you'll use.'

It went quiet for a moment.
Then Lucy giggled and said, 'It's just junk.'
'Boring,' said Jez as he opened
his mouth and yawned.

Watson flipped.
Time for his first wobbly of the day.
He raved and shouted and went on and on.
Then he walked off and left us to it. Typical.

I had to work with Jez again.
Correction.
I had to work *alone*.
Jez sulked.
He sat and played with his mobile.

OK, Jez. You play with your toy.
Maybe I can handle things better by myself.

I looked at the barrels.
I rolled four of them into one of the pools.
They floated side by side in the muddy water.
Four would be perfect for a balanced raft.

I stepped into the pool.
The water came up to my shoulders.
I lifted two planks across the top
of the barrels.
I began to tie them together with the rope.
But they began to move apart.
So I moved everything to a big patch of weed
at the edge of the pool.
Then I could push against the weed.

The move made it much easier.
I tied two planks on tightly with the rope.
Two more planks would fix
all four barrels together.
Then we'd have a perfect raft.

Before I could do any more,
Jez got bored with his mobile.
And that's when everything went wrong.

3

_____

Jez stepped on to the raft.
He had his mobile in his hand
and he'd taken off his life jacket.
'Look out, Jez.
Those two planks aren't tied on yet,'
I shouted.
'They're still loose.
Don't tread on—'

Jez looked at me as if I was a dog's dinner.
He took one more stride forward
on the loose planks.
One stride too many.

The next moment,
one of the planks tipped up.
The look on Jez's face changed.

He lurched forward.
Then he fell heavily into the muddy pool.
Suddenly I wanted to laugh.
It was so crazy.

It went quiet.
Jez is a strong swimmer.
I expected him to bob up
out of the water at any second.
Maybe he'd have his mobile
clenched in his teeth.
But he didn't.

Something was wrong.
I dived into the river where Jez had gone in.
The water was thick with weed
and it was too muddy to see anything.
My arm touched something clammy.
It was Jez.

In an instant I knew he'd got tangled up
in the thick weed.
For another split second,
I wanted to let him drown.

Swim away.
Leave him.
I didn't owe him any favours.
Why should I help him?
He'd never ever helped me.

That's what flashed through my mind.
But my heart said something else.

My hand reached down to grab him.
I pulled and yanked and tugged.
The next moment,
his head was out of the water.
I pushed him up and over
one of the fixed planks.
Then he spluttered and coughed
and wheezed.
And his eyes opened.

13

4

I looked at Jez's slumped body.
I was ashamed.
Could I really have let him drown?
How could I have ever done that?

He lay across the plank,
still coughing and crying.
We were alone in the pool.
Tariq, Lucy and Ben were in the other pool.
They were busy arguing
about making their own raft.
There was no sign of Watson.
Nobody had seen what happened.

'I'd better get some help,' I said.
Jez grabbed me.

'No,' he said. 'I'm OK.'
'You don't look OK,' I said.

Then he sat up.
'Why didn't you have
your life jacket on?' I asked.
'I don't want Watson to know about it,'
said Jez.
'You'd better not tell him.'

It went quiet. Jez let go of me.
'Why do you treat me like rubbish?'
I said.
Jez looked away.

'Why don't you call me
by my proper name?' I asked.
He didn't answer.

'You'd better put your life jacket
back on,' I said.
'Watson's bound to check up on us soon.'

I carried on making the raft alone.

5

Watson was checking the rafts.
We all stood around Ben, Tariq and Lucy's raft.
'What do you call this mess?' said Watson.
Lucy began to giggle.

'It's a mess,' said Watson.
'Just look at it.
The planks aren't fixed on properly
and you've only used one barrel.
How will you float in this?'

'Easy,' said Lucy.
'OK,' said Watson.
'Time to test it out.
Off you go, you three.'

Tariq protested.
Ben was silent.
Lucy laughed.
But Watson made them test out the raft.

It was too small for them
and it broke up in seconds.
They all finished up falling in the pool.
Then they swam about
with their life jackets on.

Watson gathered everyone around our raft.
'Did you two make this?' he asked.
I looked at Jez and he looked at the ground.

'It's brilliant,' said Ben.
'Yes, it is,' said Watson.
'So brilliant that you two can race it
through the rapids.
The rest of us will watch you do it.'
Then he gave us two paddles.

Thanks, Watson. I needed that.
Like I needed a kick in the bum.

6

Our raft floated slowly on the river.
We put our paddles gently
in and out of the water.

I don't want to do this.
I'd sooner be anywhere else.
The dentist's chair, even.
Or doing homework all day.

Jez swung his paddle high up in the air.
Then he brought it down with a thwack.
Again and again he swung his paddle.
Faster and faster went the raft.

'Let's get to the action,' he shouted.
'White water, here we come.'

'Not too fast,' I shouted.
'The raft isn't very strong.'
'Yes it is,' shouted Jez even louder.
'It's a brilliant raft.'
Maybe the raft will break up.
The knots in the rope will slip.
The planks slide loose.
The whole thing break up.

Yes.
Let it happen before the rapids.
Please …

7

There was a crack and a crunch.
'The planks are sliding,' I shouted.
'Better slow down.
Steer into the side of the bank.'

Jez turned his head towards me.
He looked hard at me.
'You're scared, aren't you?' he said.
'You know I am,' I answered.

'Relax,' he said.
'I'll sort it.
You've done all the hard work
making this thing.'

Was this Jez talking?
What had got into him?

'You sit right in the middle of the raft.
Grip the planks if you have to.
Leave it to me.
OK?' he said.

I stared at him.
'OK, Harry?' he said.

Did I hear right?
Did he call me 'Harry'?

Before I could answer,
we hit the first rapid.
Jez gave an excited wild scream.
I moved to the middle of the raft.
I threw away my paddle in the white water.
Then gripped the planks with all my strength.

We went quicker and quicker.
White water all around us.
Soaking spray.
Jolting and spinning and swirling,
but always forwards.

Up on the river bank,
high above our heads,
all the rest were running
and cheering.
Even Watson was clapping his hands
and waving.

That's when I saw it.
A giant rock ahead of us.
Right in the centre of the rapid.
Where had it come from?
There was no way round it.
We'd crash the raft for sure.
Smash it into tiny pieces.

Up on the bank,
everyone had stopped running.
Watson was pointing and shouting.

Jez had seen the rock, too.
He sat at the very front of the raft
and held his paddle high in the air.
On and on we went.
Faster and faster.

Into the path of the rock.
Nothing could save us.
Now only the rock was before us.

We lurched on.
No way through.
'Get down, Jez,' I shouted.
'You'll hit the rock.'

Jez wasn't listening.
He reached up even taller.
His paddle high in the air.
Only the black, sharp rock was higher.

The rapid pulled us suddenly to the left.
In that split second Jez made his move.
He swung the paddle hard
into the edge of the rock.
Then he pushed with all his strength.

It was a small wooden paddle.
Softer than rock,
and much smaller.
But it was enough.

The side of the raft
skimmed the edge of the rock.
The planks creaked
and the rope knots groaned.
But we were through.

All danger behind us.
Jez and me.
What a team.